# 100

## THINGS TO DO IN

# SALT LAKE CITY

## BEFORE YOU

# DIE

# 100

## THINGS TO DO IN
# SALT LAKE CITY
## BEFORE YOU
# DIE

• • • • • • • • • • • • • • • • • • • • • • • •

## JEREMY PUGH

REEDY PRESS

Library of Congress Control Number: 9781681060262

ISBN: 2015957472

Design by Jill Halpin

Cover Image: Matt Crawley

Printed in the United States of America
16 17 18 19 20    5 4 3 2 1

Please note that websites, phone numbers, addresses, and company names are subject to change or cancellation. We did our best to relay the most accurate information available, but due to circumstances beyond our control, please do not hold us liable for misinformation. When exploring new destinations, please do your homework before you go.

# DEDICATION

To Stuart Graves who loves SLC more than anyone
possibly could and Jennifer Bigler who finally came
home to help me with this book.

# CONTENTS

• • • • • • • • • • • • • • • • • • • • • • • • •

# PREFACE

Salt Lake City has always been a unique, even peculiar place. Home to the world headquarters of the Church of Jesus Christ of Latter-Day Saints (the LDS Church or, informally, the Mormons), the LDS pioneers came to Salt Lake in 1847 after a long and dangerous trek across the Great Plains. Once they arrived, they literally built this city.

For a long time, that's pretty much what most folks knew about Utah, but slowly and quietly the old Salt Lake City began to give way to what I call new Salt Lake City. As with any place so richly steeped in history, to understand the roots of change you have to go way, way, way back. In the late 1800s, federal troops stationed in Utah discovered rich veins of copper and silver and paved the way for the age of the silver barons and outside influence. The east-west railroad brought an influx of laborers who would add diversity in both faith and Mormon-defined vice to the mix, and Utah's admission to the United States in 1896 brought even more changes. Still, Utah remained apart with a dominant religion, which often dictated politics and individual conscience. Those old mining claims would become privately owned ski resorts, and the jet set had a reason to skip Colorado. Finally, the 2002 Winter Olympics cast aside the veil and shone a light on it all—Mormons, gentiles, sinners, and saints—at the base of a vast outdoor playground.

• • • • • • • • • • • • • • • • • • • • • • • •

Salt Lake City is the center of it all. A clean, walkable, bike-able city with a progressive city government, our city attracts talented and creative people from all over the world, who see Salt Lake City as a blank canvas. The food scene has exploded, as has the nightlife. Art, music, and creativity are flourishing in what was once considered a sleepy backwater.

It's an amazing time to live in Salt Lake City. A sense of energy and optimism prevails that is fueled by the imposing Central Wasatch Mountain Range that towers over our city and is essentially our communal backyard. Salt Lakers are an active bunch. We hike, we bike, we climb, we ski, we snowboard, and that mountain culture affects just about every aspect of life here.

The list in this book is by no means comprehensive. Salt Lake City itself occupies only a small area of the larger Great Salt Lake Valley and Wasatch Front and Back, so not necessarily everything on this list applies for an SLC zip code. After more than twenty years of watching and writing about this evolving and changing place, however, it represents what I think is an essential checklist to appreciate the 801. I'd love to hear what you think and of your adventures as you move through the list. You can find me @100thingsSLC and @saltlakeeditor on Twitter.

Happy travels!
Jeremy Pugh

# ACKNOWLEDGMENTS

First, I would like to thank Shawn Stinson at Visit Salt Lake, who recommended me to Reedy Press for this project.

I'd also like to thank Mary Malouf and David Nelson, whose cleventh-hour comments and reads saved you, dear reader, from not so good writing (like that).

I owe a deep debt of gratitude to all my Salt Lake friends and colleagues who chimed in with ideas for this book. I am surrounded by people who love living in Salt Lake City, and their vibrant participation in everything our city offers helps make this a wonderful place. To everyone who has given me the outlets to write about this city and state for more than a decade (*Salt Lake* magazine, Visit Salt Lake, *Sunset*, *SKI Magazine*, and *Ski Utah* magazine), thank you. The work these publications and boosters do to highlight and curate the best of life here elevates everybody's game and contributes to the quality of life in Utah.

To photographer Adam Finkle, many thanks for sharing your vast image library with me.

Finally, to Jennifer Bigler, this thing would have crashed and burned without your love and support. You're the best, Biggs!

# FOOD AND DRINK

# GET DINNER FIXINGS
## AT THE DOWNTOWN FARMERS MARKET

The Downtown Farmers Market is a social occasion and a weekly Saturday morning ritual for most Salt Lakers (and their dogs). Try not to forget that actual farmers are there selling gorgeous fruits, vegetables, and more. You'll also find producers of cheese, local meats, a juried selection of crafts, and booths filled with yummy immigrant cuisines. Carefully curated, everything at the market is locally grown and made. Go early to beat the crowds, and pick up fresh produce, a loaf of bread, a wedge of cheese, and invite all the friends you saw at the market over for Saturday night dinner.

Downtown Farmers Market
*June through October*
Historic Pioneer Park, 300 S 300 W, Salt Lake City
slcfarmersmarket.org

# OTHER FARMERS MARKETS AROUND THE VALLEY

**Murray Farmers Market at Murray City Park**
*July through October*
200 E 5200 S, Murray, murray.utah.gov

**Wasatch Front Farmers Market at Gardner Village**
*Saturdays through October*
1100 W 7800 S, West Jordan
wasatchfrontfarmersmarket.org

**Sugar House Farmers Market at Sugarmont Plaza**
*July through October*
2232 S Highland Dr., Salt Lake City
sugarhousefarmersmarket.com

**Wasatch Front Farmers Market at Wheeler Farm**
*June through October*
6351 S 900 E, Salt Lake City
wasatchfrontfarmersmarket.org

# TAKE A MAGICAL MYSTERY TOUR
## (OF SUSHI)

Dinner at Takashi is a no-reservations affair; you'll wait your turn like every other hungry sushi aficionado, but boy is it worth the wait! The fish is as fresh as you'll find at four thousand feet above sea level (flown in daily), and you'll find Takashi Gibo behind the sushi bar most nights of the week. Beautiful cuts of sashimi are a must as is a tour of the kitchen menu (don't miss the aptly named "Ridiculously Tender Flank Steak"), but Takashi's inventive and sublime rolls are the main event. Such creative concoctions as "Strawberry Fields" and the "Sgt. Pepper" (Gibo is a big Beatles fan) are subtly done and contrast with the overdone rolls cluttering the American sushi landscape. Also try the "T & T" roll and its accompanying "Hotter Than Hell" sauce, which is as advertised.

Takashi, 18 W Market St.,Salt Lake City
takashisushi.com

# BELLY UP
## AT BAR-X

For old Salt Lakers like myself, Bar-X is a storied place, once a dive bar serving "both kinds" (Bud and Bud Light) of beer in giant schooners. Back then, it was a peanuts-on-the-floor joint that catered to a grim clientele and infamously refused to serve women until the late 1980s. In 2011, however, new owners (including actor Ty Burrell, who plays Phil Dumphy on TVs *Modern Family*) arrived and turned the dank watering hole into, well, an "upscale" dank watering hole. Now meticulously crafted cocktails are served with painstaking care in a speakeasy-style lounge. In a nod to the former bar that was, you can still get a giant schooner of beer, but nobody really does anymore.

Bar-X, 155 E 200 S, Salt Lake City
barxsaltlake.com

# EAT AT THE HOME
## OF "KILLER MEXICAN FOOD"

The world-famous home of "Killer Mexican Food," Red Iguana, lives up to the hype. The hot spot run by the Cardenas family serves up Oaxacan cuisine in a wild environment, lined with punky bric-a-brac. The late, great Ramon Cardenas was a lover of music, and the walls feature signatures and autographed shrines to Carlos Santana, Los Lobos, ZZ Top, and Alejandro Escovedo to name just a few. Red Iguana is still a stop for rock 'n' rollers passing through (Lady Gaga once famously ordered ninety tacos for her crew as takeout on the way out of town.), and the food . . . Mmm. Red Iguana has the requisite burritos, tacos, and enchiladas, but venture further on the massive menu and you'll find authentic Mexican soups, lovely meat preparations, and a selection of different moles made the hard way, every day, by Red Iguana's dedicated crew.

Red Iguana, 736 W, North Temple
Red Iguana 2, 866 W, South Temple
rediguana.com

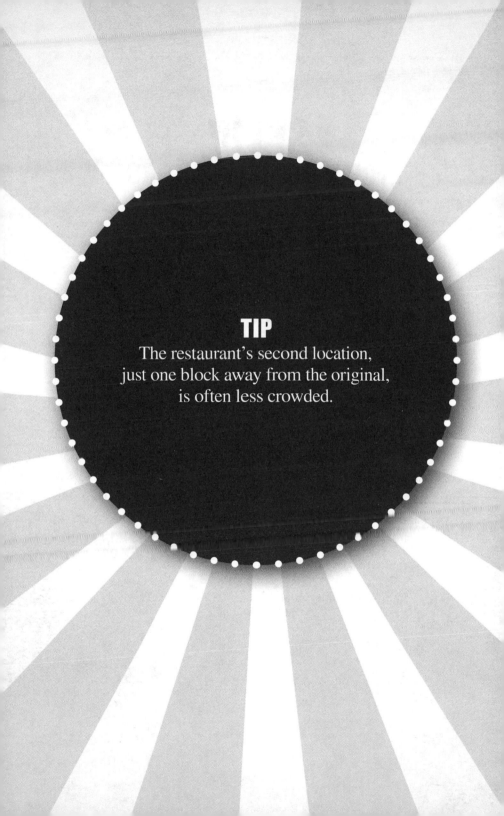

**TIP**
The restaurant's second location,
just one block away from the original,
is often less crowded.

# SKI IN
## FOR A WHISKEY TASTING

When David Perkins was looking around for a place to begin his career as a distiller of fine whiskey, Utah was not first on his list. Not only did our famously teetotaling state not have any distilleries, but there was also some question as to whether or not it was even allowed under Utah law. So he dusted off the Utah Code and found that not only were distilleries allowed, they had also been a major part of Utah history. The settling Mormons had sold whiskey to wagon parties headed through the territory en route to the West Coast. In 2009, Perkins applied for and received the first license to distill spirits in Utah since the 1870s. Now his award-winning, small-batch ryes and bourbons are prized bottles in the whiskey world, and High West can boast the world's only ski-in, ski-out whiskey-tasting room at the bottom of Park City's Town Lift (which also has a package store, open on Sundays). High West's main distillery in nearby Wanship is also worth a day trip—the facility offers tours, tastings, and whiskey workshops.

High West Distillery and Saloon, 703 Park Ave., Park City
highwest.com

# HOIST A TANKARD
## AT BEER BAR

A sister to her swankier neighbor Bar-X, Beer Bar is a rowdier affair. Long picnic tables in the style of a German beer garden stripe the wide room. Behind the bar you'll find a crew that takes its beer seriously, serving a pilsner in a pilsner glass, a lager in a lager glass, and, well, you get the idea. With a rotating cast of draughts on tap and an even more impressive selection of bottled brews from around Utah, the United States, and the world, Beer Bar is Salt Lake's finest spot to quaff a stein. Cut the alcohol with a daring selection from local butcher/magician Frody Volgger's cured meat preparations, from traditional wurst to the delicious chicken and apple sausage.

Beer Bar, 161 E 200 S, Salt Lake City
beerbarslc.com

# WALK INTO THE WOODS
## FOR A DINING ADVENTURE

You'll bundle up at Solitude Mountain Resort's base area, strap on snowshoes, and take a walk through the snowy woods as the last sun of the day dwindles to twilight. At the end of the path lies the snow-covered Solitude Yurt. Shake off the snow, hang your coat, and wrap your fingers around the hot toddy that greets your arrival. It's time to dine. The one-seating-a-night experience is a feast in all the appropriate ways. A parade of chef-chosen delights come from the rickety kitchen and are created in full view of your communal table. The wine flows, and strangers become friends in the warm confines of the round Mongolian-style yurt. For your stumble back to reality, headlamps and a friendly guide lead the way to bed and the promise of another day on the mountain.

Solitude Yurt, 12000 Big Cottonwood Canyon, Entry 2, Solitude
skisolitude.com/village-dining/the-yurt

# QUAFF A CRAFT BEER
## (AND UNDERSTAND THE FINE PRINT)

Craft beer in Utah comes with an asterisk, owing to unique liquor laws: beer that contains four percent alcohol by volume (or 3.2 by weight—it's confusing, we know) can be sold in grocery stores and on tap. Higher-alcohol brews are all bottled or canned and must be sold at liquor stores and at bars and restaurants. What does all this mean? Better brews. See, Utah beer makers brew a wide range of top-notch craft beers at all alcohol levels and routinely win big at the Great American Beer Festival. That said, the two-tiered system means our brewmasters can't just cover up mistakes by pumping up the alcohol content when they brew at four percent for taps and grocery store sales. Basically, making a craft beer in Utah requires more craft.

### UTAH'S BEST BREWERIES AND BREWPUBS
#### Epic Brewery
Specializing in high-point beers, Epic's tasting room on State Street also includes a package store selling cold beer (the beer sections in liquor stores aren't refrigerated, so this is a bonus).

What to try: Spiral Jetty IPA

825 S State St., Salt Lake City

epicbrewing.com

#### Utah Brewers Cooperative (Squatters and Wasatch)
The two granddaddies of Utah brewing banded together a few years back to distribute their popular beers. The cheeky Greg Schirf, who once famously dressed like an early American colonist and dumped kegs of beer into the

Great Salt Lake to protest high alcohol taxes, founded Wasatch. Squatters, in comparison, is a more staid, but still solid brand. Both make great beer that's easily found on tap handles and in stores around the state.

What to try (Squatters): Full Suspension Pale Ale

What to try (Wasatch): Polygamy Porter

1762 S 300 W, Salt Lake City

utahbeers.com

### Bonneville Brewery

An upstart located near the shores of the Great Salt Lake, Bonneville's mad-scientist brewer, Dave Watson, makes a lovely range of beers from his brewery in the western wilderness. You'll find his work on tap handles at the All-Star bowling chain (the brewery's owner) or after a worth-it drive out to their brewery and restaurant in Tooele.

What to try: Antelope Amber Ale

1641 N Main St., Tooele

bonnevillebrewery.com

### Bohemian Brewery

Perfect after a day of skiing in Little Cottonwood or Big Cottonwood Canyons, the hop-trellised brewery in Midvale serves beer crafted in the Bavarian tradition (and served in appropriately giant steins). They're also an early adopter of canned beers sold around Utah.

What to try: Cherny Bock Schwarzbier

94 E Fort Union Blvd., Midvale

bohemianbrewery.com

### Red Rock Brewing Co.

The flagship is the downtown gastropub, but Red Rock's award-winning beers are also sold at a package store on 400 West.

What to try: Fröhlich Pils (happy pills, get it?)

Beer store, 443 N 400 W, Salt Lake City, 801-214-3386

Brewpub, 254 S 200 W, Salt Lake City

redrockbrewing.com

# EAT A BURGER
## IN THE OLDEST BAR IN UTAH

Don't mind the stuffed St. Bernard head on the wall (no, that's not a bear; it's really a deceased dog), and do mind the ancient graffiti carved on every wooden surface. You've in the Shooting Star, Utah's oldest watering hole. Located in the scenic Ogden Valley, a trip to the Shooting Star dovetails well with a summertime exploration of the beautiful valley. The famous Shooting Star burger comes with a split knockwurst (your call). In the wintertime, skiers heading home from Powder Mountain and Snowbasin stop in for a burger and beer. Join them for a taste of Utah history.

Shooting Star Saloon, 7350 E 200 S, Huntsville
shootingstarsaloon.com

# EAT FUNERAL POTATOES
## AT THE GARAGE ON BECK

Funeral potatoes are another Utah inside joke. The cheesy, casserole-style potatoes are often served at funerals and other large church and family gatherings, but the gooey, calorie-heavy tubers, often topped with crunchy corn flakes or potato chips, are downright delicious. The roadhouse bar, Garage on Beck, has fun with the local fare by frying them up into croquette-ish bites. Additionally, the Garage is one of the best spots for live music, and enjoying Sunday brunch on its friendly backyard-style patio is not to be missed. Also try: grandma's pot pie.

Garage on Beck, 1199 Beck St., Salt Lake City
garageonbeck.com

# TAKE YOUR TEA
## AT THE GRAND AMERICA

Utah's grandest hotel, the Grand America, lives up to its name. Ornate almost to a fault, the Grand serves up its British-style tea service every afternoon for two seatings, at 1:00 and 3:30. Professor Henry Higgins himself would have no quarrel with the down-to-details event, complete with all proper English accoutrements and fussy service. He might quibble about the servers' accents, however. Pick up a sweet to go at the exquisite pastry shop La Bonne Vie.

Grand America Hotel, 555 S Main St., Salt Lake City
grandamerica.com/dining/afternoon-tea

# WOLF DOWN A PASTRAMI BURGER
## AT CROWN BURGER

Crown Burger is a local chain of chargrilled burgers and home to the pastrami burger, a quarter pounder topped with a wad of smoky meat. Meat on meat, if you will. Several copycats can be found in SLC, but the original is the best. Although famed LA food critic Jonathan Gold traces the concoction's origin to Southern California, it has taken root here in Utah. This is the burger expat Utahns hunger for.

Crown Burger, 377 E 200 S, Salt Lake City
crown-burgers.com

Other pastrami burger joints
Apollo Burger, 950 W 1700 S, Salt Lake City
apolloburgers.com

B&D Burger, 222 S 1300 E, Salt Lake City
banddburgers.com

Greek Souvlaki, 404 E 300 S, Salt Lake City
greeksouvlaki.com

# YODEL ALONG
## AT SNOWBIRD'S OKTOBERFEST

The annual Oktoberfest at Snowbird Resort is a great chance to get up into the mountains before the snow flies. Starting in September, owing to the cooling temperatures in the high-mountain setting, the festival features the requisite oom-pah-pah bands, lederhosen, and, of course, beer. Snowbird's summertime activities, zip lines, alpine slide, and mountain coaster are open for business as is the iconic Snowbird Tram. It's a nice way to wind summer down, sit in the sun and hoist a stein, eat a bratwurst, and shop the trinkets in the vendors' area.

Snowbird Center, 9385 S Snowbird Center Dr., Snowbird
snowbird.com/events/oktoberfest

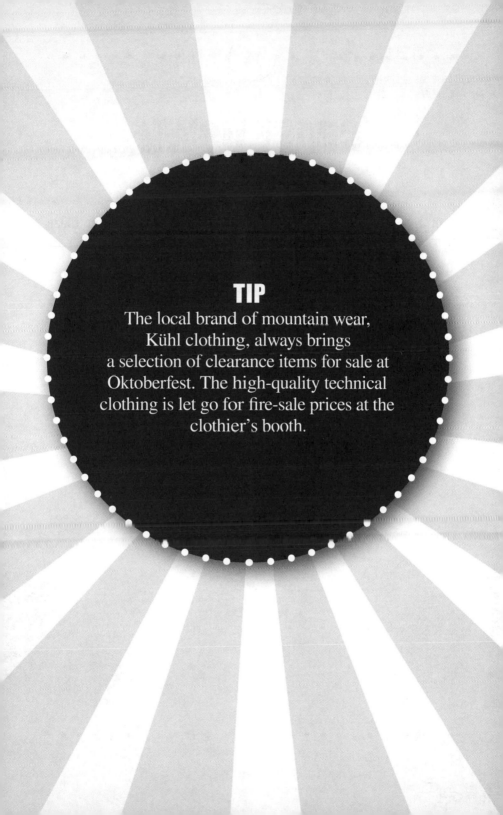

## TIP

The local brand of mountain wear, Kühl clothing, always brings a selection of clearance items for sale at Oktoberfest. The high-quality technical clothing is let go for fire-sale prices at the clothier's booth.

# CHASE DOWN
## A FOOD TRUCK

Salt Lake's weekly gathering of food trucks at Gallivan Plaza is a central space to sample the best of SLC's food truck fare, from 11 a.m. to 2 p.m. on Thursdays. You can also check out Roaminghunger.com/slc to locate the food truck near you and follow your favorites on Twitter and Facebook to get daily updates on where they'll be parked each day. Another truck assembly occurs at the Soho Food Park, which gathers regulars Monday through Saturday for lunch and dinner. Heaters in the winter, umbrellas in the summer, and tables. Follow @sohofoodpark on Twitter to get a daily lineup and plan your lunch break.

Food Truck Thursdays, 11 a.m.–2 p.m.
Gallivan Center, 239 S Main St., Salt Lake City
thegallivancenter.com/events.html

Soho Food Park, 4747 S Holladay Blvd., Holladay
Roaminghunger.com/slc
facebook.com/sohofoodpark

# FAVORITE FOOD TRUCKS

Chow Truck, Asian fusion tacos and sliders
chowtruck.com

Cup Bop, Korean BBQ
facebook.com/Cupbop

Waffle Love, Belgian waffles
waffluv.com

Kotako, Korean tacos
facebook.com/kotakotruck

Fat Kid Mac 'n' Cheese, decadent mac and cheese
fatkidmacncheese.com

Chop City, an all-pork, all-bacon serving food truck. Yes!
facebook.com/chopcityslc

# EAT A BRIGHAM CITY PEACH
## ON FRUIT WAY

Take a drive north on I-15, get off the freeway at the Willard exit, and get on Utah Highway 89. This is the southern tip of the famed "Fruit Way," where you'll discover roadside produce stands featuring the best of the state's growing season, including the luscious Brigham City peach. The famous peaches are celebrated every year in September during the northern town's annual Peach Days Festival. Although the beautiful peaches are sort of the star of Utah's produce pantheon, many fruit and vegetable festivals can be found around the state that offer pleasant helpings of small-town charm and low-rent pageantry to celebrate the cornucopia of Utah's growing season.

# JUNE

**Strawberry Days, Pleasant Grove**
strawberrydays.org

# AUGUST

**Bear Lake Raspberry Days, Garden City**
gardencityut.us/rasberry-days-2011

**Corn Festival, Enterprise**
enterprisecornfest.wix.com/enterprisecornfest

**Trout and Berry Days, Paradise**
paradise.utah.gov/trout-and-berry-days-2015

# SEPTEMBER

**Golden Onion Days, Payson**
paysonutah.org/news_events.oniondays.html

**Peach Days, Brigham City**
peachdays.org

**Melon Days, Green River**
melon-days.com

# OCTOBER

**Apple Fest, New Harmony**
newharmonyfire.com/apple.htm

# ORDER UP
## SOME LION HOUSE ROLLS

The Lion House was occupied by Salt Lake's founder and perhaps most famous resident, Brigham Young. Located on the LDS Church Headquarters grounds, adjacent to another of Brigham's stately homes (the Beehive House), the Lion House is a reception hall and restaurant (called the Lion House Pantry). The warm, fluffy rolls, traditionally part of many Salt Lakers' Thanksgiving celebrations, are its signature menu item and a walk by the place in the morning as the rolls bake inside will have your stomach growling. The Lion House Pantry is open six days a week.

Lion House Pantry, 63 E South Temple, Salt Lake City
templesquare.com/lion-house

# CREEK-SIDE BRUNCH
## AT RUTH'S DINER

Ruth's Diner opened in 1930 and is a classic roadside diner with a lovely and bucolic patio on the bank of Emigration Creek that draws the brunch crowd in droves every weekend. Ruth herself was a tough old broad, who was known for not looking at IDs too hard. "They can enforce their own laws," she once said, and until she sold the restaurant in 1977, it had a smoking section (i.e., wherever Ruth was smoking). She lived behind the restaurant until she passed away in 1989 at the age of 94, but her legend lives on. Don't miss the mile-high biscuits and the famous chocolate pudding.

Ruth's Diner, 4160 Emigration Canyon Rd., Salt Lake City
ruthsdiner.com

# YOU WANT FRY SAUCE WITH THAT? YES. YES, YOU DO.

In Utah, the acquisition of fries comes with a question: You want fry sauce with that? To the uninitiated, the question is befuddling. What is this fry sauce? Well, it's basically ketchup and mayonnaise, sometimes with a mystery ingredient (often relish and cayenne pepper) whirled together into a creamy, pink concoction. The ketchup-to-mayo ratio varies from establishment to establishment, and the particular calibration of the mix is a matter of individual taste. It's hard to say who has the best fry sauce; it is, after all, a pretty simple condiment, but I've found that Hires Big H serves up an excellent emblematic cupful. Some folks in fancy places try to sneak it onto your plate by calling it "aioli," but we know. Dude, that's just fry sauce in a ramekin.

Places to try the fry sauce:
Hires Big H, 425 S 700 E, Salt Lake City
hiresbigh.com
Crown Burger, 377 E 200 S, Salt Lake City
crown-burgers.com

# EAT A FAMOUS PASTRY
## AT LES MADELEINES

Pastry chef Romina Rasmussen created a national food sensation when she started making kouign amann at her shop Les Madeleines more than a decade ago. The kouign amann is a flaky, sweet, savory pastry from the Brittany region of France, but the labor-intensive and butter-rich pastry wasn't done much even in Parisian bakeries. Romina perfected her recipe and reintroduced the gooey delicacy to our mouths, even though we still can't pronounce it right. Her efforts have brought national attention from such renowned publications as *Food and Wine* and *Bon Appétit*, and she has been featured on the Food Network's *The Best Thing I Ever Ate.* Her shop is one of Salt Lake's favorite lunch stops, serving beautifully crafted sandwiches, salads, and pastries in tranquilly civilized surroundings. Stop in for lunch and walk out with a kouign amann for dessert.

Les Madeleines, 216 E 500 S, Salt Lake City
lesmadeleines.com

# DRINK THE PERFECT
## CUP OF COFFEE

Fastidious isn't a strong enough term to describe the owner of Caffe d'Bolla. John Piquet is a *nut* for his coffee and is nationally known as a roasting and brewing expert. He positively fusses over every cup he serves. If you really want to see him in action, order a $12 cup of siphon coffee. It's an impressive procedure as he painstakingly fires up the siphon and serves you what may be the perfect cup of coffee. Don't ask for cream or sugar unless you want to see John's eyes roll completely out of his head and then be chased out of his coffee shop.

Caffe d'Bolla, 249 E 400 S, Salt Lake City
caffedbolla.com

# GET A FROSTY
## ROOT BEER AND A BURGER

Once upon a time Hires Big H was part of a chain started by the Hires Root Beer Company, and this last bastion of the empire is still serving amazing burgers after all these years, with a frosted mug of root beer on the side, naturally. Hires's founder, Don Hale, was a local Zig Ziglar of sorts, full of folksy wisdom, and you'll find his quotable witticisms around the restaurant and can even buy a book of his advice on your way out. The joint still has carhop service and sells the secret recipe root beer base to make your own at home.

Hires Big H, 425 S 700 E, Salt Lake City
hiresbigh.com

# PUB CRAWL
## ON SLC GREENBIKES

Salt Lake's GREENbikes follow the mold of bike-share programs in Austin, Texas, and New York City: you check out a bike, ride to a station near your destination, and drop the bike off. It's also a great way to crisscross the city and visit bars. The GREENbike pub crawl on the following page will take you from station to station in a nice big loop around town. Always bike safely, wear a helmet, etc., and if you get too blotto, please call an Uber, Lyft, or taxi.

GREENbike
greenbikeslc.org

# PUB CRAWL

## STOP 1

**Squatters Pub and Brewery**
Bike station: Squatters Station @ the Rose
147 W Broadway, Salt Lake City

## STOP 2

**Twist Bar**
Bike station: Rocky Mountain Power Station
225 S Main St., Salt Lake City

## STOP 3

**Copper Common**
Bike station: TravelWise Station
160 E 300 S, Salt Lake City

## STOP 4

**Dick 'n' Dixies**
Bike station: 3 & 3 Uncommons Station
300 S 300 E., Salt Lake City

## STOP 5

**Beer Bar and Bar-X**
Bike station: 200 S 200 E Station
200 S 200 E., Salt Lake City

## STOP 6

**Beer Hive**
Bike station: Energy Development Station
136 S Main St., Salt Lake City

# GO TO MADDOX
## ON THE WAY TO
## GRANDMOTHER'S HOUSE

Located about an hour north of Salt Lake in Perry, Maddox Ranch House is one of those don't-miss-it, worth-the-drive restaurants. Still studded in the original '50s steak house kitsch, Maddox remains family run and is still serving families on their way to grandmother's house. The big neon sign outside boasts famous chicken, but actually it's sort of strange chicken, fried in a breading that some folks love and others, meh. Where this strange chicken-fried fry batter works best is on Maddox's chicken fried steak. The thin breading covers a patty of ground sirloin that makes it one of the menu's biggest highlights. The steaks all come from grass-fed, free-range, etc., cattle that until just a decade or so ago would graze right outside the panoramic windows. The Ranch House also has a helping of bison steaks on the menu. Every meal comes with all the trimmings, delicious rolls (with fresh-whipped raspberry honey butter), salad or seafood cocktail, and your choice of potato on the side, as is tradition. The pies are to die for, and the birch root beer brewed on-site by Irv Maddox, grandson of founder Irvin Maddox, is worth the sugary calories.

Maddox Fine Food, 1900 S Highway 89, Perry
maddoxfinefood.com

# REEK OF GARLIC

The Cotton Bottom Inn is a great dive at the mouth of Big Cottonwood Canyon. In summer, the patio is filled with leather-clad bikers, and in the winter booted skiers and boarders crowd in after the lifts close each day. Its famous garlic burger is a strange creature served on a doughy hoagie roll, featuring American cheese with four garlic-powder-soaked patties, pickles, and a pepperoncini on the side. This is a standoff situation. Everybody in your party will reek of garlic for the rest of the day, so you're all in this together.

Cotton Bottom Inn, 2820 E 6200 S, Salt Lake City
cottonbottominn.com

# SLURP CHEESY SOUP
## AT THE PUB

The Desert Edge Brewery is known simply to locals as the Pub, one of the few restaurants in the Trolley Square mall (a destination in itself). The Pub is a favorite for ladies who lunch, the Paint Nite Out crowd, and Utah Utes boosters on game day—basically, classic Salt Lake. Its menu hasn't changed a bit over the years, and the cheese-laden French onion soup is a lovely treat on a cold day. Take some time to explore Trolley Square, which once served as the city's trolley barn.

Desert Edge Brewery at the Pub, 273 Trolley Square, Salt Lake City
desertedgebrewery.com

# SHOP FOR TIRES,
## EAT A TAMALE

Victor's Tire Shop and Custom Wheels provides the services its name indicates on Salt Lake's west side. It's also a restaurant serving amazing tamales and other Mexican cuisine. You order at the tire service counter and wait for your order in a hastily added on addition with a few tables, salsa bar, and soda fountain. This is not gringo Mexican. It's the real deal, and beyond the beautiful tamales you'll find authentic posole and other homemade delicacies.

Victor's Tires, 851 W 1700 S, Salt Lake City
victorstires.net/Restaurant.html

# AFTER YOU SKI,
## APRÈS-SKI

The tradition of an after-ski-day beverage is ensconced in Utah's ski and snowboard culture. Sometimes the thrill of spending a day in the high mountains, gliding on the greatest snow on earth is rivaled by that pleasant feeling of plopping down on a stool in a rowdy bar or cozying up by the fire in a fancy lodge and ordering a beer and a shot (or a preciously concocted cocktail) as the sun sets on the mountain. Here are my favorites for each of the nine (nine!) resorts within an hour of Salt Lake City:

## ALTA SKI AREA
**Alta Peruvian Lodge Bar**
Loud, rowdy, and fun, with colorful memorabilia from seventy-five-plus years of Alta history all over the walls.
**Rustlers Lodge**
A snifter of brandy will do at this cozy spot to warm yourself by a roaring fire.

## SNOWBIRD
**BYOB to the Tram Deck**
Bask in the sun at this hub of activity at Snowbird. Locals bring up small backpacker-style propane stoves to mix up hot toddies after a day on the steeps.

## BRIGHTON
### Molly Greens
Inside this classic A-frame ski chalet, you'll find the best pile of nachos in Utah and a pint of Cutthroat Ale waiting for you.

## SNOWBASIN AND POWDER MOUNTAIN
### Shooting Star Saloon
Located in the valley below both resorts, crowd into Utah's oldest watering hole for a pitcher of Coors and a Shooting Star burger.

## SUNDANCE
### Owl Bar
Belly up and sip a shot of whiskey at the restored 1890s wooden bar. It was moved from the Rosewood Bar in Thermopolis, Wyoming, to Sundance, Utah. The Rosewood was frequented by Butch Cassidy's Hole in the Wall Gang.

## SOLITUDE
### The Thirsty Squirrel
A local favorite—order a brew and sprawl out at this comfy lounge in the Solitude Village.

## PARK CITY MOUNTAIN
### The Corner Store Pub & Grill
Propane heaters warm a convivial and rowdy patio scene featuring $1 PBRs and hot wings.

## DEER VALLEY
### The St. Regis Bar and Lounge
Enjoy the famous Bloody Mary or glass of fine wine around the fire pit on the patio.

# MUSIC AND ENTERTAINMENT

# STROLL THROUGH
## THE TWILIGHT CROWD

The youth-centric Twilight Concert Series lights up Salt Lake's central core throughout the summer. Roving packs of cyclists and teens teem through the streets on the way to and from the concerts, and the shows themselves in Pioneer Park skew toward the hip, featuring such bands as St. Vincent, the Black Keys, Beck, and other indie types. Although the event is supposed to be about the music, getting close to the stage is a young man's game, and thus the shows become, more than anything, a place to see and be seen. Most of us just mingle in the back, enjoying the beer and food trucks. Tickets are a mere $5. They used to be free, but overcrowding at a Modest Mouse show in 2010 gave organizers a scare.

Pioneer Park, 350 S 300 W, Salt Lake City
twilightconcerts.com

## TIP
Stop into the Tin Angel for a preshow dinner. Former SLC punkers Jerry Liedtke (Chef), Kestrel Liedtke (Heart), and Robin Kilpatrick (Soul) throw down a locally sourced menu of tasty food in a singularly cool atmosphere located right across from Pioneer Park.

# BONUS TIP

The Salt Lake City Bike Collective bike valet service is free during the shows. Pedal down to the park and drop off your bike in the secure holding pen. Bonus, bonus tip: Duck out of the show a little early to avoid long waits for your bike. Leave a tip though. The valet service is a fund-raiser for the collective, which helps put thousands of kids and working poor on bikes every year.

Tin Angel, 365 W 400 S, Salt Lake City
801-328-4155, thetinangel.com

# SEE A SHOW
## AT URBAN LOUNGE

This small, not-a-bad-spot-in-the-house music club is the place to see bands in Salt Lake on the way up the ladder of fame and stardom. The spartan club with cheap beer presents an eclectic lineup of acts, from twee indie bands to death metal wizards and hip-hop kings pretty much seven nights a week. Urban Lounge shows start late, and the bands that play there inevitably return to play the small, informal space that lets you get right up front.

Urban Lounge, 241 S 500 E, Salt Lake City
theurbanloungeslc.com

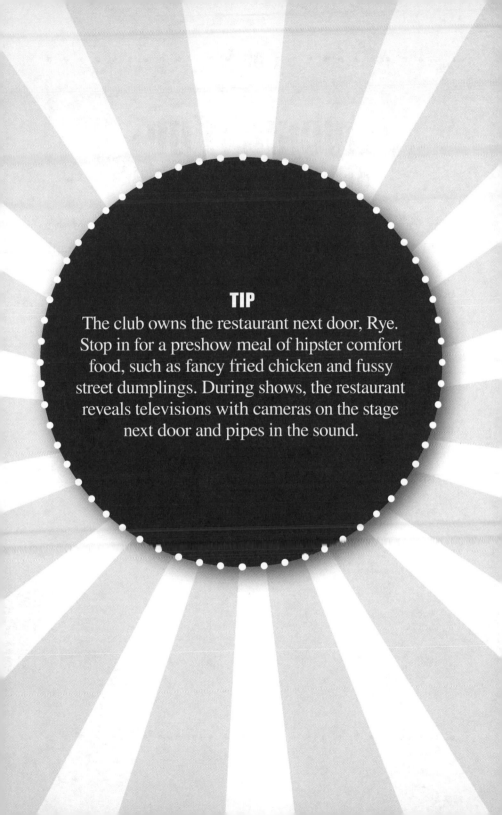

## TIP

The club owns the restaurant next door, Rye. Stop in for a preshow meal of hipster comfort food, such as fancy fried chicken and fussy street dumplings. During shows, the restaurant reveals televisions with cameras on the stage next door and pipes in the sound.

# PICNIC IT UP
## AT A RED BUTTE SHOW

This lovely amphitheater situated in the eastern foothills of the Salt Lake Valley is the setting for a signature Salt Lake moment: a great concert in a great setting. There isn't a bad seat in the house, and a liberal picnic policy that allows your own food and drink makes this a social scene. In fact, there's a whole culture of folks who get up there early and wait for the gates to open at 6 p.m. to rush in and throw down the blankets. Red Butte books excellent midrange acts, such as David Byrne, Alabama Shakes, and Jason Isbell, to name just a few. The concerts run from May into September and often sell out. Beyond the amphitheater is the beautiful Red Butte Garden, a large botanical garden for strolling through before and during the show.

Red Butte Garden, 300 Wakara Way, Salt Lake City
redbuttegarden.org/concerts

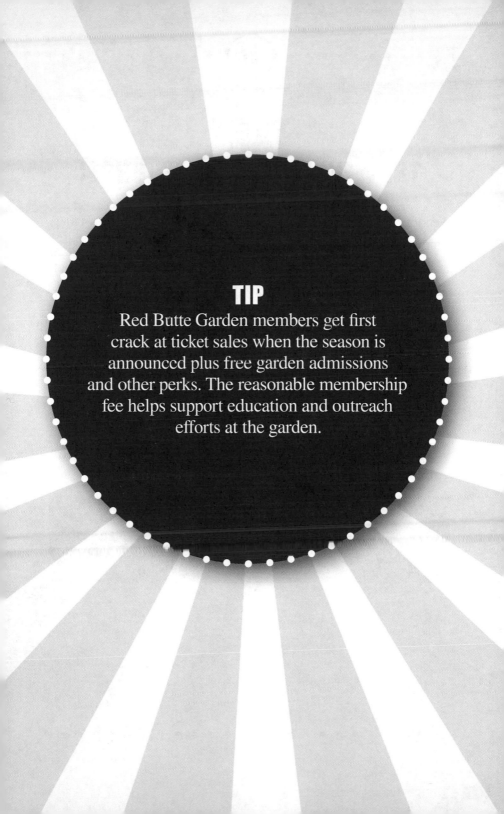

## TIP

Red Butte Garden members get first crack at ticket sales when the season is announced plus free garden admissions and other perks. The reasonable membership fee helps support education and outreach efforts at the garden.

# TAKE
## THE WENDOVER FUN BUS (ONCE)

Wendover, a dumpy town over the state border that divides Utah's saints and Nevada's sinners, is spruced up just enough to draw us west but not great enough to make us stay. It's about ninety minutes away from Salt Lake City proper, and the over-the-border casinos run a weekly "fun bus." The bus is cheap and a fun ride out, especially with a convivial group of friends. The coach "host" feeds you drinks and plays silly bingo games. The ride back is a grim affair; the bus departs at 2 a.m. from Wendover, putting you back in SLC around 4 a.m.

wendoverfun.com/resort/daily_bus_trips
lebus.com/pickup-locations

### TIP
Despite the snark, Wendover does have one truly redeeming spot: the concert hall at the Peppermill Casino. It's a beautiful hall that brings in a range of B- to C-list acts that are often worth the drive, or fun bus.

# SEE A SHOW
## AT KILBY COURT

This all-ages venue is an institution. A whole generation of disenfranchised Salt Lake youth found themselves at Kilby and along the way witnessed the growth of the Salt Lake indie scene. Many major bands have passed through the Court on their way up the indie music ladder (Iron and Wine, Deathcab for Cutie, Neon Trees, Fall Out Boy), and the small space, hidden down an alley on Salt Lake's west side, still remains a placc for youngsters to discover great new music and be a part of something larger than homework and high school. Don't worry. It's not just for kids (although they are there). It's truly a unique spot to hear music.

Kilby Court, 741 S Kilby Court, Salt Lake City
kilbycourt.com

# TUNE INTO THE SOUNDTRACK OF LIFE
## IN SALT LAKE

The beloved community radio station KRCL, with its eclectic mix of music and progressive community involvement, is the constant backbeat to life in Salt Lake. It's playing in our cars, our workplaces, and around the house—pretty much constantly. Take, for example, a typical chore-filled Saturday. The day opens up with coffee and Shannalee's *Saturday Breakfast Jam*, followed by Grateful Dead–laced deep tracks on Dave Santivasi's *Saturday Sagebrush Serenade* (including a mediation for world peace every week at noon). The day moves along with Courtney's *Afternoon Delight,* a quirky three-hour mix of indie, new wave, old soul, and new rock, and you'll be putting away the tools while Robert Nelson's *Smile Jamaica* plays his trademark "all killer, no filler" three-hour block of reggae and dub music. Weekdays, it's mornings with Ebay, lunchtime with Eugenie, and drive time with Bad Brad. In a world of boring commercial radio stations, homogeneous satellite radio, and computer algorithms programing our listening, KRCL is a beautifully human blend of music and activism and an essential part of living the good life in Salt Lake.

KRCL 90.9 FM
1971 W. North Temple
krcl.org

# SPEND THE DAY
## AT LAGOON

The wooden roller coaster, known simply as "the roller coaster," is the foundation of an excellent un-themed amusement park thirty minutes north of Salt Lake. The rickety old coaster hearkens back to Lagoon's turn-of-the-century origins, but the modern park features all manner of whirligigs and geegaws to fling you and your crew about every which way. The sprawling one-hundred-plus-acre park also includes a water park (bring your swimsuit), a zoo (accessed by a goofy train that runs around its namesake lagoon), and a Pioneer Village, complete with authentic pioneer buildings and a daily shootout show at high noon.

Lagoon, 375 Lagoon Dr., Farmington
lagoonpark.com

# VISIT THE STATE ROOM

Salt Lake's music scene got a shot in the arm when longtime Red Butte promoter Chris Mautz and his partner Darin Picoli founded the State Room in 2009. The well-designed space is dedicated to its acoustically beloved sound stage. Inside the theater are no tawdry beer signs or anything really to distract from the stage, which is fronted by a roomy dance floor and backed by tiered seats for those who like to have a seat. The bar out front offers a civilized coat check, an efficient bar staff, and reasonably priced drinks. The State Room is only open for shows—a range of midlevel to big bands in a wonderfully intimate space that puts live music first.

State Room, 638 S State St., Salt Lake City
thestateroom.com

# LAUGH
## ALONG WITH THE LOYAL OPPOSITION

For more than forty years, the Salt Lake Acting Company (or earlier versions thereof) has been producing an annual send-up of Utah politics and church culture called *Saturday's Voyeur*. The name is an arcane reference to a schlocky piece of '70s-era Mormon musical theater called *Saturday's Warrior*. The show is rewritten every year from headlines and news of the weird, which, in Utah, is low-hanging fruit. The campy production—filled with inside jokes, parodies of popular songs, wacky plots, and caricatures of local politicians, church leaders, and news-making figures—is a way for the loyal opposition to blow off steam after suffering through another year of exasperating politics in Utah. The summertime performances are a convivial affair (that is, BYOB).

Salt Lake Acting Company, 168 W 500 N, Salt Lake City
saltlakeactingcompany.org

# SEE THE STARS
## AT THE CLARK PLANETARIUM

Space is cool, and the Clark Planetarium has plenty of it—three floors of exhibits for the little Neil Armstrong in all of us. Its heart and soul is the star show planetarium called the Hansen Dome, a state-of-the-art, 360-degree projection system that goes way beyond the field trip star shows of your childhood. (It also has, of course, the requisite late-night Laser Zeppelin and Floyd shows to help you remember your forgotten college years.) The Clark is also home to an IMAX theater showing blockbuster films in the biggest format on earth as well as more educational fare.

Clark Planetarium at the Gateway, 110 S 400 W, Salt Lake City
clarkplanetarium.org

# RENT *RUBIN AND ED*
## AT THE TOWER THEATRE

The Tower Theatre is the flagship of the Utah Film Society, a Sundance venue during the independent film festival, and where you'll find showings of all the foreign films, esoteric documentaries, period pieces, and more Helen Mirren vehicles than you'd ever want to see. The theater's lobby also has a collection of rare and hard-to-find DVDs that you won't find on Netflix or Amazon. Do yourself a favor and rent *Rubin and Ed*, an out-of-print movie filmed in Utah in the early '90s. Starring Crispin Glover and Howard Hesseman, the oddball buddy flick is about, umm, two guys going out to the desert to bury a frozen cat.

Tower Theatre, 876 E 900 S, Salt Lake City
saltlakefilmsociety.org

# "HALLELUJAH"
## ALONG WITH THE UTAH SYMPHONY

Come Christmastime, the Utah Symphony performs Handel's *Messiah* for a glorious sing-along in Abravanel Hall. The jubilant event is one of the hot tickets of the holiday season. You know the chorus, right?

Abravanel Hall, 123 W South Temple, Salt Lake City
utahsymphony.org/15-16-season/special-events/1109-messiah-sing-in

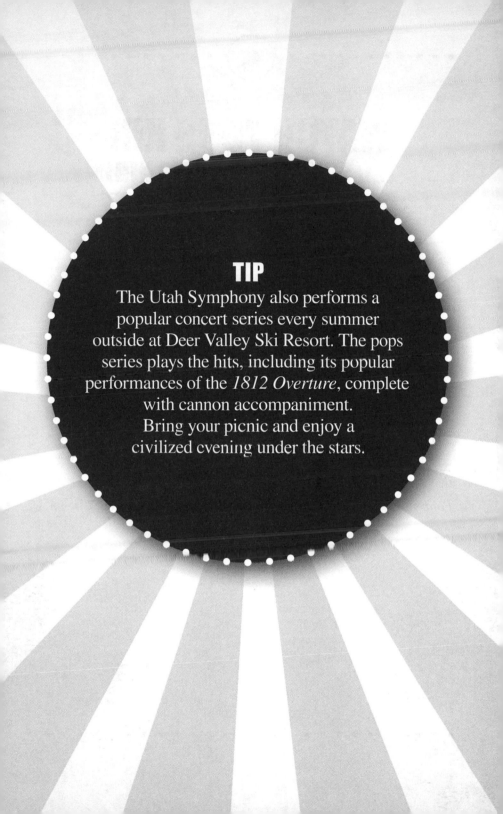

## TIP

The Utah Symphony also performs a popular concert series every summer outside at Deer Valley Ski Resort. The pops series plays the hits, including its popular performances of the *1812 Overture*, complete with cannon accompaniment. Bring your picnic and enjoy a civilized evening under the stars.

# WATCH YOUR KID
## (OR YOUR NEIGHBOR'S KID)
## DANCE IN *THE NUTCRACKER*

Ballet West is one of the oldest ballet companies in America and continues to mount challenging works of ballet and modern dance, but every tiny dancer dreams of dancing with the Sugar Plum Fairy, right? Each year thousands of aspiring young dancers audition for the right to play a part in the annual performances of *The Nutcracker* at the Capitol Theatre, alongside company members and guest professionals. Additionally, Ballet West also produces a satirical version of the famous ballet called *The Nutty Nutcracker*. The annual just-for-yucks production pulls its jokes from the previous year's collection of pop culture winners and losers (including, one year, making fun of Ballet West's inclusion in the reality show *Breaking Pointe*), and crams them into something loosely resembling a ballet.

Capitol Theatre, 50 E 200 S., Salt Lake City
balletwest.org

# SEE A CONCERT
## IN THE "SUPERNACLE"

The giant LDS Conference Center was built in 2000, primarily to host the Church of Jesus Christ of Latter-Day Saints's semiannual gatherings (called simply "conferences"), but many other musical and performance events are held there—namely, the free-but-hard-to-get-a-ticket-to Mormon Tabernacle Choir Christmas concerts. An engineering marvel, with insanely fastidious acoustics, the 1.4-million-square-foot center seats twenty-one thousand people and is large enough to hold two imaginary Boeing 747s side by side. The view from every seat of the house is (miraculously?) unobstructed by support pillars. You can also take a tour of the joint, including the beautiful rooftop gardens.

LDS Conference Center, 60 North Temple, Salt Lake City
lds.org/locations/temple-square-conference-center

©Utah Office of Tourism, Dan Campbell

# OUTDOORS AND SPORTS

# PADDLE OUTRIGGER CANOES
## ON THE GREAT SALT LAKE

Utah is home to many Pacific Islanders, thanks to early missionary efforts from the LDS Church in the Polynesian Islands. So very far from the idyllic shores of their homeland, a group of transplanted Hawaiians brought the traditional outrigger canoe to the waters of the Great Salt Lake and founded Hui Paoakalani, a paddling club at the GSL Marina. The club hosts the Annual Duke Paoa Kahanamoku Water Fest (Duke was an Olympic medal–winning swimmer) in June and goes out for weekly paddle sessions every Saturday from 10 a.m. to 3 p.m. from April through mid-September.

Great Salt Lake Marina, 1075 S 13312 W., Magna
huipaoakalani.blogspot.com, gslmarina.com

# DIVING IN THE DESERT?
## SCUBA AT FIVE THOUSAND FEET ABOVE SEA LEVEL

Landlocked Utah isn't a place you'd think of for Scuba diving, but we've got two of the world's most unique spots for underwater adventure—Bonneville Seabase and the Homestead Crater. Seabase is carved out of the salty earth above a natural warm mineral spring in Grantsville, Utah—quite literally in the desert near the shores of the Great Salt Lake. Seabase's main diving area, called "Habitat Bay," is stocked with tropical fish and, yikes, sharks (friendly nurse sharks). The Homestead Crater, located in Midway, is equally strange—a mineral water pool located inside a rocky caldera. In the 1990s, intrepid divers drilled into the rock to access the ninety-degree water inside and built a diving and snorkeling area. The warm, crystal-clear waters are an eerie blue, and divers can descend as far as sixty feet into the crater's depths.

Bonneville Seabase, 1600 UT-138, Grantsville
seabase.net

Homestead Crater, 700 Homestead Dr., Midway
homesteadresort.com/utah-resort-things-to-do/homestead-crater/

# ONE MINUTE OF TERROR:
## RIDE THE OLYMPIC BOBSLED TRACK

After I completed my one-minute blast down the official bobsled track of the 2002 Winter Games at the Utah Olympic Park, I thought, "I'll never do that again." This is a true bucket list item, such as skydiving or going to the top of the Empire State Building. Do it. Once. And if you can't muster the courage to sign the lengthy waiver, tamer activities are available at the Utah Olympic Park. In the summertime, the park has zip lines, alpine slides (a mini bobsled, if you will), summer tubing (yes, that's a thing), and its popular show that features the athletes of the US freestyle ski aerials team flipping and flying into the pool they use for summer training.

Utah Olympic Park, 3419 Olympic Pkwy., Park City
utaholympiclegacy.org

# HIKE TO THE "LIVING ROOM" FOR SUNSET

In the foothills above the University of Utah, a spider web of trails snakes up the hillside, a popular area used by trail runners, dog walkers, and mountain bikers. The Living Room hike will take you up to a set of rocks arranged like a sofa and chairs Fred Flintstone would appreciate. If you do make the hike for the sunset, remember to bring headlamps for the walk down in twilight.

Living Room Trailhead, 383 Colorow Rd., Salt Lake City

# CHOOSE SIDES
## IN THE "HOLY WAR"

Football rivalry takes on biblical proportions each year when the BYU Cougars meet the University of Utah Utes on the gridiron. The spirited rivalry between the state university and the LDS Church–owned private school brings up the division between Mormons and non-Mormons in an annual contest of vulgarity (Ute fans) and pious sneers (Cougar fans) that spills out across the city. The big game, for most, is a socially acceptable way for gentiles to fly their flags in the face of the dominant religion. The rivalry has diminished in importance since Utah joined the Pac-12 and BYU went the independent route in 2011, but its cultural significance remains.

Rice-Eccles Stadium, 451 S 1400 E., Salt Lake City
utahtickets.com
LaVell Edwards Stadium, 1700 North Canyon Rd., Provo
byutickets.com

## TIP

The game alternates between Salt Lake City and Provo, but the festivities are somewhat diminished at Cougar Stadium. Catch the tailgate near the Utes' Rice-Eccles Stadium for the rowdiest display of Ute pride, but if you can't get a ticket to the big rivalry game, any game day at Rice-Eccles is a must-do event in Salt Lake City.

# WALK AMONG THE WILDFLOWERS
## AT ALTA IN ALBION BASIN

July is peak wildflower season in Utah, and one of the best spots to see this annual outbreak of beauty is Albion Basin above Alta Ski Resort. The wildflower bloom depends on the weather, but traditionally its peak occurs around July 24 (Pioneer Day). Pack a picnic and make the drive up Little Cottonwood Canyon to Alta, and enjoy the meadows full of mountain daisies, Indian paintbrush, and bluebells. Pretty much the greatest hits of alpine flowers are on display every year. Try to go on a weekday, however, to avoid the crowds.

Albion Basin, Alta
Broads Fork: Mill B South Trailhead, Big Cottonwood Canyon

## TIP

If you're up for a strenuous hike and want to ditch the crowds altogether, the meadow at the top of Broads Fork is another of Utah's best wildflower areas. The hike, which starts in Big Cottonwood Canyon, is a seven-mile beast, but you'll likely have the meadow up top all to yourself.

# CHANT
## ALONG AT A REAL SALT LAKE GAME

Major League Soccer is officially a thing, and Real Salt Lake (pronounced ree-Al) is one of the best teams in the US. Watching a match (not a game, silly) at Rio Tinto Stadium is an intense experience; the twenty-thousand-seat arena throbs with the exuberance of rabid Real supporters. Adopting the traditions of the European leagues, RSL fans employ a complicated system of chants and songs to cheer on the boys in claret and cobalt. Do your homework at realsaltlake.com and you'll fit right in.

Rio Tinto Stadium, 9256 S State St., Sandy
realsaltlake.com

# LOOK
## O'ER THE VALLEY BELOW

Ensign Peak, located on the hillside behind the state capitol, is a bumpy protuberance that offers a prominent vista of Salt Lake City. The LDS pioneers used the peak to survey the valley and as a watchtower of sorts. The quick hike (great for a lunchtime break) will have you high above the city in about twenty minutes. Hiking at night, with headlamps for your climb down, ups the wow factor with the city lights stretched out below. The trailhead is at the top of a residential area above the Utah capitol.

Ensign Peak Trail, Salt Lake City
slcparks.com

# ESCAPE
## TO CITY CREEK CANYON

A true gem of escape, City Creek Canyon is mere minutes away from downtown Salt Lake City, where you can leave it all behind on a stroll up the canyon's paved road. The road goes six miles back into the foothills of Salt Lake and, apart from some water treatment facilities, is entirely undeveloped. At the top, the Salt Lake Rotary Club has built some supercool picnic areas, including one called the Grotto on the shores of the babbling City Creek. Bikes are welcome on odd days in the summer and every day in winter as well as leashed dogs. You'll find runners and bikers and walkers all taking a moment to step out of the city and find a little peace.

City Creek Canyon Rd., Salt Lake City

# "SPELUNK"
## TIMPANOGOS CAVE

A national monument, Timpanogos Cave is just an hour away from Salt Lake City. The ranger-led cave tours take place after a steep 1.5-mile hike and often sell out, so book early. The climb is worth it; the wondrous Timpanogos Cave, an ancient cavern with stunning crystals called "frostwork," and the requisite stalactites and stalagmites live up to its monument status.

UT-92, American Fork
nps.gov/tica/

### TIP
Explore the Alpine Loop—a scenic byway near Mount Timpanogos and one of the best places to enjoy the fall colors in Utah.

# TAKE A DOG
## TO DOG LAKE

Having a dog (yours or a friend's) as a hiking buddy is pretty much the rule around here, and although some of our canyons (Big and Little Cottonwood) are off-limits to canines (we get our drinking water from the snow up there), Millcreek Canyon is agnostic species-wise. You can find many great hikes in Millcreek, but perhaps none is more popular on an off-leash day (odd calendar days) than the trek back to Dog Lake. The moderately strenuous six-mile hike leads dogs and their owners to a good-sized muddy lake, where the pups can frolic while owners take their ease on the shore. Please, please, please pick up after your mutt.

Millcreek Canyon, Big Water Trailhead

# SHOOT THE TUBE

A high school rite of passage, "shooting the tube" is a thrilling ride on a raft (of some sort) through a metal culvert that runs underneath the I-15 freeway. The brave access the tube from Tanner Park. Cross the freeway on the system of shared bike and pedestrian bridges, and take a dirt trail down to an area below a giant rock pinnacle, a traditional graffiti spot charmingly dubbed "Suicide Rock," where high schoolers and college fraternities still make their marks in the eternal battle of who rules. The culvert lies at the base of the rock. Not much art is involved. Just get a sturdy floating device, such as a pool float, and hold on for dear life. You'll emerge into a large pool at the top of Tanner Park, a popular dog park.

Midway Adventure Co., Tanner Park, 2760 S 2700 E., Salt Lake City

# A SUNDAY AFTERNOON
## AT THE BALLPARK

A lazy Sunday afternoon, the crack of the bat, the quiet murmur of the crowd, a cold beer, and a dog. Salt Lake has one of the best minor league ballparks in America, and here's a secret: the Sunday day games are pretty well empty. Baseball is a pastime after all, America's pastime. The local AAA farm club of the Los Angeles Angels, the Salt Lake Bees, have good years and bad, but who cares? The ballpark looks right up at the gorgeous mountains above the city, and you won't pay much for a ticket. Sit in the sun and while away the day while the boys of summer chase their major league dreams.

Smith's Ballpark, 77 W 1300 S., Salt Lake City
saltlake.bees.milb.com

### TIP
Throughout the summer, night games are often punctuated
by fireworks displays above the ballpark.

# SCALE THE HEIGHTS
## OF MOUNT OLYMPUS

Call it an initiation or even self-imposed hazing, but the slog to the summit of Mount Olympus (9,026 feet) is a necessary ritual on the path of calling yourself a hiker in Salt Lake, where hiking, biking, and climbing are as endemic to life as navigating the subway is for a New Yorker. The grueling seven-mile-round-trip hike gains 4,196 feet in elevation, all on the exposed face of mighty Mount Olympus. It's a daunting task, and the giant rock stairs and scramble at the tippy top are a final twist of the dagger into your burning legs for sure. The reward, though, is the top-of-the-world panorama of the Central Wasatch Range and the Salt Lake Valley far, far below.

Mount Olympus Trailhead, 5800 S and Wasatch Blvd., Holladay

# RIDE UP
## EMIGRATION CANYON

Emigration Canyon is named for the Mormon pioneers who used the canyon to descend into the Salt Lake Valley. The LDS leader, Brigham Young, famously declared, "This is the place" to mark the moment when the weary pioneers emerged from the canyon to observe their new home. Nowadays, the canyon is prime real estate and lousy with road cyclists, who make the ascent to Little Mountain, at the top, in droves. It's a perfect road ride, with a wide shoulder, cyclist-conscious drivers, and a steady climb; it's the tamest of Salt Lake's canyon routes and an excellent introduction to the sport. The very top of the ride features a steep set of switchbacks that reward riders with a view of the valley below and a not-too-steep descent back down.

Emigration Canyon

# FLOAT
## THE WEBER RIVER

About an hour's drive north of Salt Lake City proper, you access the Weber River from the top of Ogden Canyon. Several guide companies offer shuttle services and tube and raft rentals, but you can really do this one on your own; plan for a shuttle car and some burly tubes that can withstand the rocks and tree branches. The two-hour float is a rowdy affair—most people bring an extra tube to float a cooler full of beer alongside—but the water itself is pretty mellow and shallow, with only a few tricky areas to navigate. You can get out and jump off rocks into deep pools in several spots, and a local landowner annually installs a giant rope swing for the truly brave souls in your flotilla.

8 E Main St., Midway, Utah

# SEE A BISON,
## EAT A BISON AT ANTELOPE ISLAND

The largest island in the Great Salt Lake, Antelope Island is another world. The arid island, accessed by a causeway from I-15, is a lovely place to roam and disappear from the city. The views from the west side of the island out across the lake are a glimpse back in time before the works of man cluttered up the scenery. What to do? Well, there's a herd of bison roaming around out there (and a restaurant that serves bison burgers sans irony), an excellent trail system, several muddy beach areas to access the salty water, and the roads are heaven for cyclists.

Antelope Island State Park is located approximately forty-one miles north of Salt Lake City. Take Exit 332 off Interstate 15, and then drive west on Antelope Drive to the park entrance gate.

stateparks.utah.gov/parks/antelope-island

# TIP

Early spring, fall, and winter are the best times to visit. Summertime is hot, and what the island offers in stark beauty is offset by a noticeable lack of shade, and then you have bugs. Brine flies are prevalent in the warmer weather and pretty awful. They bite and leave painful itchy welts. Call the park to ask if the flies have hatched. An excellent way to see the island is the annual Antelope by Moonlight Ride in July, a twenty-mile organized bike ride underneath the full moon.

antelopebymoonlight.com

# TAKE THE TRAM
## TO HIDDEN PEAK

It's a quintessential Utah thing to do, especially for non-hikers in your world. The iconic red-and-blue trams will whisk you from the tram deck up to Hidden Peak, where you'll find spectacular views of the rugged Alpine peaks of the Wasatch Range and can peer down upon Salt Lake City. The newly constructed Summit Lodge offers shelter and lunch, and the second floor's height kicks the already jaw-dropping view up another notch. In the summer, you can hike down to the base or hike into (and out of, be warned) Mineral Basin. In late June and July, the wildflowers are a riot of color and beauty.

Snowbird Tram, 9385 S Snowbird Center Drive, Snowbird
snowbird.com

## TIP

The hike up under the tram by the Snowbird trail system is a bugaboo, but the steep climb from eighty-one hundred feet to eleven thousand feet above sea level is a rewarding journey. Snowbird doesn't like to advertise this, but with a friendly wink for the tram operators you can ride down for free as a reward for making the climb.

# LEARN TO SKI
## (OR SNOWBOARD)

Salt Lake City is the base of six (six!) world-famous ski resorts (Alta, Snowbird, Brighton, Solitude, Park City, and Deer Valley). All are less than forty-five minutes from your door, and living in (or visiting) Utah and not skiing or snowboarding is like living in California and never going to the beach. We've got a skier on our license plates for heck's sake. So take a lesson. Even if you're a great skier or boarder, a lesson is a great way to tune up your technique. Do not let your boyfriend or girlfriend try to teach you. This situation is a relationship killer (believe me, I know). All six of the Salt Lake–area resorts have excellent ski school programs and affordable lessons.

skiutah.com

### TIP

January is Learn to Ski and Snowboard Month, and resorts offer deals as low as $45 for rentals, lessons, and lift tickets.

# HOW 'BOUT THAT JAZZ?

Okay, the Jazz isn't a great team. "We're in a rebuilding year" is a phrase we have been saying for maybe ten years, but memories of the glory days when the Jazz were going toe-to-toe with Michael Jordan's Bulls live on, and long-suffering Jazz fans are among the most supportive and vociferous in the NBA. They make sitting through a game, no matter how bad the Jazz are stinking, a raucous, exciting event. A word about the name: the Jazz used to be the NBA club in New Orleans. The team moved to Utah, with its Mardi Gras–laced name in 1979, and has been a charming non sequitur ever since.

Energy Solutions Arena, 301 South Temple, Salt Lake City
nba.com/jazz

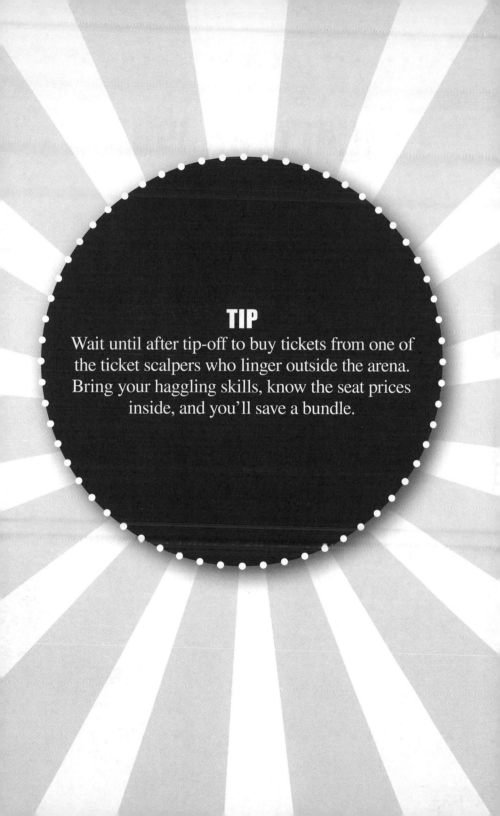

## TIP

Wait until after tip-off to buy tickets from one of the ticket scalpers who linger outside the arena. Bring your haggling skills, know the seat prices inside, and you'll save a bundle.

# THAT'LL DO, PIG,
## ERR, DOG

Remember Babe, the pig who thought he was a dog? (Don't lie. You've seen *Babe*, like, a million times.) The Soldier Hollow Classic sheepdog trials in Heber Valley are basically *Babe* without the pig. Contestants come from around the globe to show off their dog's herding skills, which are impressive even if you're not a shepherd (or a talking pig). The four-day event, one of the biggest of its kind in the world, is held over Labor Day weekend. It also features a vast array of dog-centric activities, such as the popular Splash Dogs competition, where water dogs go for distance, leaping into a pool chasing (what else?) a tennis ball. Note: Unless your four-legged friends are competing, you're asked to leave the pooches at home to avoid distracting the professionals.

2002 Soldier Hollow Drive, Midway
soldierhollowclassic.com

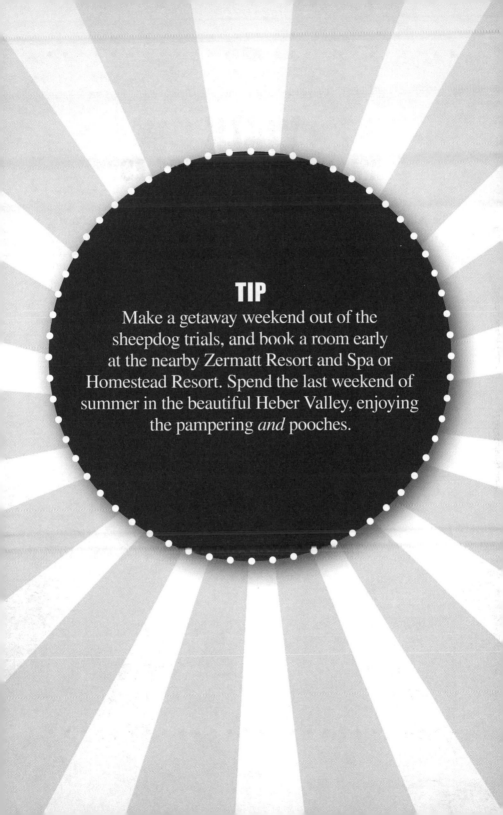

## TIP

Make a getaway weekend out of the sheepdog trials, and book a room early at the nearby Zermatt Resort and Spa or Homestead Resort. Spend the last weekend of summer in the beautiful Heber Valley, enjoying the pampering *and* pooches.

# WALK
## AMONG THE ICE CASTLES

The Midway Ice Castles are constructed each year out of soaring walls of frozen water to the delight of bundled-up adults and children who walk through the maze-like structure in droves every winter. The wondrous playground is built when the cold really sets in and is naturally weather dependent. Buy tickets in advance, get a thermos of hot cocoa, and take the kids for a cold-weather adventure.

Midway Ice Castles, 2002 Soldier Hollow Rd., Midway
icecastles.com/midway

# SKATE
## ON THE FASTEST ICE ON EARTH

Many of the records set in speed skating during the 2002 Winter Games in Salt Lake City still stand today. The Utah Olympic Oval is a training center for future Olympians, but you need not be one of those to enjoy the beautiful rink, which offers public skating as well as a great place to watch athletes in training, international speed skating events, and more. Come winter, the oval's indoor running track attracts runners who want to stay out of the cold.

Utah Olympic Oval, 5662 Cougar Lane, Salt Lake City
utaholympiclegacy.org/oval/

# CELEBRATE THE SOLSTICE
## AT THE SUN TUNNELS

Land artist Nancy Holt installed the sun tunnels in 1978 in the western desert near Lucin, Utah. The four massive concrete tubes aren't much to look at in the light of day, but during the summer and winter solstice, the tunnels frame the sun at sunrise and sunset. For each astrophysical event, a motley assemblage of nature lovers, art lovers, weirdos, and wanderers camp out around the tunnels for an all-night party to witness the events.

Sun Tunnels, Lucin

# SOAK YOUR BONES
## AT FIFTH WATER HOT SPRINGS

Enough of a hike to keep out the casual but not enough of a trek to deter interesting folks, Fifth Water Hot Springs is located in Diamond Fork Canyon. You'll hike five miles out and back to the springs, which pour into a series of pools that are hottest near the source. An excellent excursion in either winter or summer, be prepared that hot springs around the west are often clothing optional, and you may encounter a bare behind or two. Feel free to bare your own.

Fifth Water Hot Springs, Diamond Fork Canyon

# ROAD TRIP
## TO RED ROCK COUNTRY

Southern Utah's stunning red rock deserts are the exact opposite of the north's mountainous landscape. Salt Lake City is within five hours' drive of some of the world's most amazing places of solitude and splendor. You're not a real Salt Laker until you've ducked out of work early on a Friday (don't let them hear your keys jingling), loaded up the car, and made the trek down south for the weekend. In addition to the five national parks within Utah's borders, there are numerous state parks and national monuments, lovely little towns, and miles of wide open spaces. Here are some highlights:

## MOAB
**Distance from SLC: 234 miles**
A base of operations for exploring nearby Arches and Canyonlands National Parks as well as Dead Horse Point State Park. Moab is also close to the famous (and dangerous) Slickrock Trail mountain biking area.

## GOBLIN VALLEY STATE PARK
**Distance from SLC: 223 miles**
This state park is home to a preponderance of red rock "goblins." The mushroom-like products of incomplete erosion create a wondrous maze of weirdness to wander through.

## SPRINGDALE
### Distance from SLC: 307 miles
This cute little town is the entrance to Zion National Park and a great base for exploring the region. Nearby St. George and Cedar City offer year-round golfing (St. George) and the Tony Award–winning Utah Shakespeare Festival (Cedar City).

## BOULDER, ESCALANTE, AND SCENIC HIGHWAY 12
### Distance from SLC: 306 miles
Bryce Canyon and Capitol Reef National Parks as well as the Grand Staircase–Escalante National Monument are all along this off-the-beaten path roadway. Don't miss a reservations-required dinner at the famous Hell's Backbone Grill in Boulder.

## LAKE POWELL
### Distance from SLC: 383 miles
Formed by Glen Canyon Dam, this reservoir has more miles of knotted-up coastline than the western edge of the United States and is a strange watery oasis in the middle of the harsh desert.

# CULTURE AND HISTORY

# CAMP OUT
## FOR THE PARADE

The Days of '47 is the annual celebration of Pioneer Day (July 24), the day the LDS settlers entered the valley. The annual parade on or around that date, depending on when the weekend falls, is a Utah tradition. Families camp out on the parade route to ensure a prime spot. The parade is, well, a parade, but the camping is a wholesome all-nighter on the city streets, and this isn't just chairs and blankets; people go big, with generators, blow-up mattresses, and much more.

daysof47.com

# GET A DOSE
## OF "UTAH WEIRD" AT
## GILGAL SCULPTURE GARDEN

Gilgal Sculpture Garden was the backyard of Thomas Battersby Child Jr., a businessman and mason who died in 1963. The bizarre folk art sculptures dot a quiet little park nestled in a Salt Lake neighborhood. The themes are often LDS centric, notably the giant phinx bearing the likeness of LDS Church founder Joseph Smith. The park is open to the public daily.

Gilgal Sculpture Garden, 749 E 500 S., Salt Lake City
gilgalgarden.org

# SEE
## HISTORIC TEMPLE SQUARE

On July 24, 1847, the weary Mormon pioneers arrived in the Salt Lake Valley, but their leader, Brigham Young, didn't let them rest long. They got busy, real busy. Just four days after they arrived, they marked the spot to build the Salt Lake Temple. Construction took forty-six years, and early Salt Lake City grew up around it. Now you can say, literally, that all roads lead to Temple Square (the city's grid system counts out on the compass points from here). The iconic, granite-spired structure is the centerpiece of the grounds that pack in some of Utah's densest history lessons. There's a lot to do at Temple Square, as well as the adjacent LDS Church Headquarters Plaza and Conference Center, but at a minimum take an hour and stroll through the beautiful, intensely manicured grounds. It is—whatever your faith, creed, or culture—a place of peace in the heart of the city.

Temple Square, 50 North Temple, Salt Lake City
lds.org/locations/salt-lake-city-temple-square

# TEMPLE SQUARE MUST-DOS

### Hear the Pin Drop

The historic Mormon Tabernacle, in use since 1898 and home to the Mormon Tabernacle Choir, is an acoustic marvel. Tours include the famous pin drop, in which your group can clearly hear a pin being dropped up front while standing in back.

### Tour the Beehive House

One of Brigham Young's stately homes is open for tours. Yes, Brigham was a polygamist, and his homes had many, many rooms for his many, many wives. Take the tour and be rewarded with a glimpse into Utah's peculiar past and a taste of what pioneer candy tasted like (not good).

### Go to the 26th floor

Once the tallest building in Salt Lake, the LDS Church office building is the worldwide administrative headquarters of the church. An observation deck on the 26th floor offers a commanding view of the city and a unique view of the top of the Salt Lake Temple.

### Hear the Mormon Tabernacle Choir for free

Every Sunday morning the Mormon Tabernacle Choir is featured in a live devotional broadcast called *Music and the Spoken Word*. Tickets to the weekly broadcast are free. The broadcast location switches between the original historic tabernacle in the winter and the larger LDS Conference Center (we call it the "Supernacle") during summer to accommodate larger crowds.

### Here Comes the Bride(s)

Young LDS Church members are directed to marry as a matter of doctrine, and the ceremony is held within the temple. Sit in the Main Street Plaza and watch the parade of modest young couples posing for postnuptial pictures on the temple's steps.

### See the Christmas Lights

On the day after Thanksgiving, the Christmas lights come on at Temple Square, and it just wouldn't be the holidays without a stroll through the lights. They start stringing the millions of lights in August, and the display is a sparkly celebration of the season.

# SEE THE STARS
## AND MAYBE A GREAT FILM AT THE SUNDANCE FILM FESTIVAL

The big show happens in Park City, where celebrities promoting their films are often sighted clomping around historic Main Street in hastily purchased winter clothes. Although the star-stalking thing is a thing, let's remember that Sundance is one of the world's most important independent film festivals. A cinephile's dream, the two-week festival is a buffet of films both little and big and always interesting. Although the crowds flock to Park City, film lovers know to stay down in Salt Lake, where the wait is tolerable, and the celebrity circus is less prominent.

sundance.org/festivals/sundance-film-festival

# TIP

The Trolley Square box office posts a daily list of what tickets they have available each morning. Pick up a ticket to a Salt Lake theater and play film roulette.

# FEEL THE NEED,
## THE NEED FOR SPEED

The Bonneville Salt Flats are really, really flat and dense. The salty substrate makes the surface especially suited for crazy people who are attempting to set world land speed records. Each year in September these enthusiasts gather for the World of Speed event to test their mettle and engineering skills on the flats—driving the fastest cars in the world, with top speeds of four hundred miles an hour, in their quest to become the fastest humans on Earth. Yeah. Crazy.

saltflats.com

# MARCH PAST THE MANSIONS
## ON SOUTH TEMPLE

One of Brigham Young's prescriptions for a healthy economy was forbidding his followers to seek out gold and other minerals in them thar hills. Remember, the LDS pioneers came here in 1847, and the California gold rush was in 1849. Brigham's logic was based on what he believed was the boom-bust nature of mining-based economies. Thus, it was left to outsiders to discover the wealth under the soil, and they did. In the late 1800s, a group of capitalists tapped into a rich vein of silver in the area that is now Park City, and they became very, very rich. The "silver barons," as they were called, built massive mansions on South Temple Street, one of which now serves as the Utah governor's home. Take a walk down the long tree-lined avenue.

South Temple between State St. and Virginia Ave.

# WAVE A RAINBOW FLAG
## IN THE UTAH PRIDE PARADE

Being the world headquarters of a conservative church brings out the oppositional defiance in nonbelievers. That tension, at times acrimonious, makes Salt Lake City a surprisingly liberal place despite its location in the heart of one of the reddest states in the Union. In 2015, Salt Lake voters elected Jackie Biskupski the city's first openly gay mayor. The Salt Lake Pride Festival is perhaps the best example of this jubilant opposition, and the four-day festival is one of the largest of its kind in the nation (seriously). The celebration brings LGBT folks and their loving supporters out into the streets and culminates in a joyous parade through the heart of the city that rivals the annual Pioneer Day parade in participation and attendance.

utahpridefestival.org

# FLY THE HELICOPTER
## AT DISCOVERY GATEWAY

Discovery Gateway is a children's museum, but then again "museum" is too boring a word. Think interactive exhibits and hands-on play areas that cater to kids and the kid inside all of us. The sixty-thousand-square-foot, multifloor play space features engaging workshops and programs, all centered around kid-powered fun. They also have this supercool helicopter on the roof, where you can pretend to rescue people and also this place where you can pretend to be on the news. And then you can pretend to go to the store and buy all the groceries. It's way awesome. Can we go? Can we go? Pleeease?

444 W 100 S., Salt Lake City
discoverygateway.org

# MARVEL
## AT *SPIRAL JETTY*

American sculptor Robert Smithson built *Spiral Jetty* in 1970. The giant sculpture on the northern tip of the Great Salt Lake is what it says it is—a curly rock jetty that goes out into the lake. During wet years, the jetty is covered with water, but of late the beautiful rock sculpture is bone dry with a salty patina.

*Spiral Jetty*, Corinne, UT 84307

# TIP

A trip out to *Spiral Jetty* is paired well with a
visit to the Golden Spike National Historic Site,
which commemorates the coming together of the
eastern and western lines of the transcontinental
railroad at Promontory Summit in 1869.

Golden Spike National Historic Site
6200 N 22300 W., Brigham City, nps.gov/gosp

# LEARN
## FROM MASTER DA VINCI

Named after the original Renaissance man, Leonardo da Vinci, the Leonardo (or Leo for short) is a unique space that examines the intersection of science, technology, and art. The hands-on learning space offers an ever-changing mix of exhibits designed to engage the mind and lift the heart, and it's not just for kids. The Leo also serves as a venue for public debate and gatherings and presents evening events, such as the "Leo after Dark" series for adults that present food and wine tastings, food chemistry classes, trivia nights, and more.

The Leonardo, 209 E 500 S., Salt Lake City
theleonardo.org

# TIME TRAVEL
## AT THE NATURAL HISTORY MUSEUM OF UTAH

The museum's interactive exhibits walk you through life in Utah—from rocks on up to the flora and fauna—and make it a standard educational field trip. The building itself is also reason enough for a visit. Its architecture recalls the slot canyons and rocks of southern Utah, and following the winding path through the museum takes you on a journey through the natural history of our state. But, yay! Dinosaurs! Lots of dinosaurs. Utah is one of the world's richest areas of dinosaur fossil discovery, and the museum is home to impressive exhibits of skeletal giant reptiles from way, way back.

Natural History Museum of Utah, 301 Wakara Way, Salt Lake City
nhmu.utah.edu

# CHECK THE SKYLINE
## WEATHER REPORT

The Walker Center, built in 1912, is one of Salt Lake's grand old edifices. Its distinctive lighted top broadcasts a weather report every evening. Put down your phone, look up, and use this key to the code: blue = clear skies, flashing blue = cloudy skies, red = rain, flashing red = snow.

Walker Center, 175 South Main St., Salt Lake City

# GO UP (DOWN?)
## GRAVITY HILL

The one-way road that runs around the edge of the mouth of City Creek Canyon is a strange optical illusion that is a source of whimsy, especially for bike riders who use the road's large bike lane. The road seems that it's going downhill, but you'll be pedaling hard because you're actually going uphill. The opposite effect occurs on the western side of the road.

Gravity Hill, City Creek Canyon Rd., Salt Lake City

# TRIP OUT
## IN MEMORY GROVE

One of the best movies about our city is the 1998 independent film *SLC Punk!* The charmingly funny, oddball picture follows the lives of two misfit punks in the 1980s. One of its most famous scenes is an acid trip scene in Salt Lake's Memory Grove, a park at the mouth of City Creek Canyon containing a variety of historical monuments and memorials. While you should probably skip the illegal drug use, the park is a secluded little oasis in the city filled with trails, nooks, and crannies to explore.

Memory Grove, 75 N 120 E., Salt Lake City
slcparks.com

# HYDRATE
## WITH HISTORY

When the Mormon pioneers arrived in the Salt Lake Valley, finding water was top of mind. Early on, a natural spring was discovered at what is now the corner of Salt Lake's best urban green space, Liberty Park. The spring was corralled into a drinking fountain that runs year-round and is a refreshing treat after a run in the park or a game of tag on the grassy knoll. Explore the rest of the park, and be sure to notice the Seven Canyons Fountain, which will give you an excellent sense of the valley's topography. Also check out the Live Action Role Players (LARPers) who practice their broadsword skills on the grass.

Liberty Park, 600 E 900 S., Salt Lake City
slcgov.com/cityparks/parks-liberty-park

# FIND THE
# TWO-HEADED LAMB
## AT THE DUP MUSEUM

The Daughters of Utah Pioneers Museum on Capitol Hill is a great place to learn the history of the women and families who, in many cases, literally walked across the Great Plains to settle Utah in 1847. The museum tells a gentler side of that history and gives a glimpse into what family life was like on the trek. It's also (whaaa?) the home of a strange taxidermied two-headed lamb. Happy hunting!

Daughters of Utah Pioneers Museum, 300 Main St., Salt Lake City
dupinternational.org

# DISCOVER THE "PLACE"
## AT THIS IS THE PLACE STATE PARK

You may have guessed that the Mormon settlement of Salt Lake City is a very big deal around here, and apart from Temple Square, perhaps the most important LDS history site is This Is the Place State Park. A monument marks the spot that Brigham Young intoned the famous words and allowed his followers to finally park their wagons and handcarts. You can just imagine the collective sigh of relief. The park has historical buildings, a trove of history, and docents who practice such lost arts as blacksmithing, woodworking, and more. Kids can play pioneer games (that are pretty fun, actually).

This Is the Place State Park, 2601 E Sunnyside Ave., Salt Lake City
thisistheplace.org

# CLIMB THE STAIRS
## AT THE SALT LAKE CITY PUBLIC LIBRARY

Oh, man, our library. Designed by internationally acclaimed architect Moshe Safdie, the city library is a beautiful public space: the soaring main hall, the beautiful plaza with fountains, the light streaming in the plentiful windows. The grand steps encircle the eastern flank of the building, and a walk up the stairs offers a lovely view of the city as well as access to the library's rooftop gardens (with a resident beehive). Take the glass elevator back down and look at books, read a magazine, work on the free Wi-Fi (I wrote much of this book on the library's third floor), browse the library shops, or just slow down and enjoy this wonderful space.

Salt Lake City Public Library, 210 E 400 S., Salt Lake City
slcpl.org/branches/view/Main+Library

# LOOK UP
## FOR FLYING OBJECTS

Salt Lake's city center is dotted with an ongoing public art project called *Flying Objects*. The whimsical sculptures are installed on poles near Salt Lake's main cultural halls. A local favorite is Brook Robertson's *Zion/Alien Rocky Mountain Alliance 4.4* at the Rose Wagner, which features a pair of LDS missionaries behind the wheel of a Jetsons-style flying saucer.

Abravanel Hall: 10 S West Temple, Salt Lake City
Rose Wagner Performing Arts Center: 125 W 300 S., Salt Lake City
Capitol Theatre: 15 W 200 S., Salt Lake City

# SEE A SILENT FILM
## WITH FULL ORGAN ACCOMPANIMENT

The Edison Street Events Center, historically known as the Organ Loft, is home to a full-on Wurlitzer theatre pipe organ that was once state of the art in movie soundtracks. The reception hall offers periodic showings of silent film classics, accompanied by the magnificently maintained organ. The most popular of these is the annual October showings of *The Phantom of the Opera*.

Edison Street Events Center
3331 S Edison St. (145 E.), Salt Lake City
edisonstreetevents.com

# SHOPPING AND FASHION

# DIG THROUGH THE DESIGNER SECTION
## AT NPS

A through-the-looking-glass close-out, scratch and dent, ultimate end of the road for any item that was once sold for full price somewhere in the world, NPS (standing generically for National Product Sales) is a clearance sale, every day, but in the middle of this daily fire-sale chaos is a special designer section. These are real deals, not knockoffs—Coach bags, Jimmy Choo shoes, TAG Heur watches. The selection changes constantly (except for some very odd decorating items that will be there forever). You pretty much have to pick through everything, but once in a while you'll pay insane prices for that perfect dress, watch, shoes, or umm, heirloom cuckoo clock?

NPS, 1600 Empire Rd., Salt Lake City
npsstore.com

# SINK INTO THE OFURO BATH
## AT THE KURA DOOR

The Kura Door, a Japanese-infused spa in the Salt Lake Avenues neighborhood, is great for that take-me-away day, but its signature Ofuro bath is the best of the menu. Let's just say that when it's over you may not remember what day it is or who's president. Your bath agent will take care of the details, and just remember to have someone pick you up afterward. Kidding, sort of.

The Kura Door, 1136 3rd Ave., Salt Lake City
thekuradoor.com

# UPGRADE YOUR SPECS
## AT THE SPECTACLE

For more than three decades, Salt Lakers who sport glasses have known to look here for that special pair of specs. Remember the signature glasses worn by Elvis that you probably just call "Elvis glasses"? Owner John Cottom designed those as well as the heart-shaped eyewear famously worn by Ann Margret. His handiwork can also be seen in the sci-fi classic *Blade Runner*. Plus lots of cool vintage glasses and hard-to-find designer brands.

Spectacle, Trolley Square, 602 E 500 S., Salt Lake City
thespectacle.com

# ORDER
## A BESPOKE SUIT

Back in the day (like 1905), Utah Woolen Mills was a mill, an actual textile manufacturer that had a fleet of straw-hatted and fedora-sporting salesmen dispatched around the country to hawk its finely woven woolen goods. As the twentieth century charged on, the family-run store morphed into a retail outlet that kept the emphasis on fine goods. Today, the fifth and sixth generation of the Stringham family runs the store that *Esquire* magazine shouted out as one of the best gentlemen's outfitters in America.

City Creek Center, 59 W South Temple, Salt Lake City
utahwoolenmills.com

# KEN SANDERS
## RARE BOOKS

Ken Sanders Rare Books is one of those special places that can only exist because of the personality of its owner. Ken Sanders is a counter culture icon in Utah. His locally focused rare and used bookstore is a veritable museum of Utah history and a repository for the works of such great Utah writers as Wallace Stegner and Edward Abbey, but it's also so much more. His store holds a wonderful collection of old maps, rock 'n' roll concert posters, and postcards from fin de siècle Salt Lake City.

Pop into the delightfully musty old bookstore and most days you'll find the bearded and gruff ol' Ken Sanders holding court from his comfy easy chair. See him flex his expertise on *Antiques Road Show*.

Ken Sanders Rare Books, 268 S 200 E., Salt Lake City
kensandersbooks.com

# GET LOST
## IN DECADES

It's almost like the staff who stalk the floor at Decades Vintage Clothing love their beautifully curated collection of threads so much they'd rather you *not* buy it, but their brisk service is part of the charm of this sprawling store on State Street, where you'll find a treasure trove of midcentury gems, jewelry, hats, shoes, and much more. The staff's aloof nature tells you that this place isn't about playing dress up; it's about fine goods and timeless fashion.

Decades, 627 S State St., Salt Lake City

# ANARCHY
## IN SLC

Salt Lake City, unexpectedly, was heavy into the punk thing during the Reagan era. While most of the country was rehabbing at Betty Ford and marching lockstep into the new "morning in America," the scruffy underground was busy saying "no" to saying "no," breaking things, and being generally mad and loud. Salt Lake City upped this anti-everything vibe with an extra sheen of squeaky-clean Mormon and bred an especially virulent antibody to the cultural vaccine, *SLC Punk!* Two vestiges of this period live on at Raunch Records and the Heavy Metal Shop (motto: "Peddling evil since 1987"), selling vinyl and angry memorabilia from back in the days of anarchy in SLC.

Raunch Records, 1119 E 2100 S., Salt Lake City
Heavy Metal Shop, 63 S Exchange Pl., Salt Lake City
heavymetalshop.com

# SHOP
## AT NINTH AND NINTH

Ninth and Ninth is a cool neighborhood shopping and dining area anchored by the Tower Theatre. You'll find hipster clothing shops; the town's highest-end bike shop, Contender; and the Children's Hour, the little gem that sells smart books and toys for the kids as well as hard-to-find designer clothing brands and gifts for mom. Stop into Zuriick for a pair of handmade shoes and a haircut and head into Cahoots for whimsical gifts and adult toys. Take a lunch break at Mazza, serving Lebanese cuisine, or East Liberty Tap House, serving beer and hipster food.

900 S 900 E., Salt Lake City
9thand9th.com

# SCORE A DEAL
## AT THE SUNDANCE CATALOG OUTLET STORE

C'mon. Your coffee table has an earmarked Sundance catalog on it, right? The catalog, featuring unique clothing, jewelry, and housewares inspired by Robert Redford's haute western aesthetic, has an outlet store here in Salt Lake. This is a true outlet; the markdowns are legit and often steep.

Sundance Catalog Outlet Store, 2201 S Highland Dr., Salt Lake City
sundancecatalog.com

# WINDOW SHOP
## AT UTAH'S TIFFANY

Utah's original jeweler has been putting beautiful baubles on people for nearly a century, and even if you're not in the market for fine jewelry, stopping into its flagship store on State Street is worth the trip. The store is located in the former Salt Lake City Public Library Building, beautifully renovated into a gorgeous store filled with gorgeous jewelry.

OC Tanner Jewelers, 15 S State St., Salt Lake City
octannerjewelers.com

# BE A KID AGAIN
## IN JITTERBUG ANTIQUES & TOYS

Crowd into a delightfully curated consignment store of retro goods and an impressive menagerie of toys and games from days of yore. With its windup tin toys, Jitterbug Antiques is a chattering, whimsical wonderland and an excellent spot to find nostalgia-chumming gifts.

Jitterbug Antiques & Toys, 243 E 300 S., Salt Lake City

# DESERET
## INDUSTRIES

While you probably think of Goodwill or the Salvation Army when you think thrift store, we in Utah think Deseret Industries. Known as the D.I., this store has many locations around the valley, and diving through the stacks of clothes, books, housewares, and everything else is a rite of passage for college students furnishing their first apartment. Gems can sometimes be found amid the piles of polyester jumpsuits.

deseretindustries.org

# DISCOVER
## THE QUILTED BEAR

Handicrafts are part of the Mormon pioneer tradition; quilting, cross-stitch, knitting, and other homespun hobbics arc all zcalously pursued here in Utah. The Quilted Bear, with locations around the valley, is the showcase for local artisans and crafters who sell their wares at the eclectic stores, which also sell crafting supplies. If there is such a thing as Mormon decor, this is the spot to see it on display.

The Quilted Bear, 111 E 12300 S, Draper
quiltedbear.com

# SUGGESTED
## ITINERARIES

## MORMON UTAH

## WEIRD UTAH

# FAMILY FUN

# ACTIVITIES
## BY SEASON

Salt Lake City is a place with four clear seasons, some of the activities are season-specific or at their best during a particular time of year.

## SPRING

## SUMMER

# INDEX